Let's Start Writing!

Your Name: _ _ _ _ _ _ _ _ _ _ _

We should brush our teeth

twice a day.

We should brush our teeth

twice a day.

The Sun is a big ball of

fire.

The Sun is a big ball of

fire.

Eat healthy food.

Eat healthy food.

Do not waste food.

Do not waste food.

Do not waste water.

Do not waste water.

Eat balanced diet.

Eat balanced diet.

I love to dance.

I love to dance.

Do not tell a lie.

Do not tell a lie.

Butterfly comes out of its

pupa.

Butterfly comes out of its

pupa.

Willow trees grows near

water.

Willow trees grow near

water.

Help others as much as

possible.

Help others as much as

possible.

grandfather knows many

riddles.

grandfather knows many

riddles.

My father is a great

teacher.

My father is a great

teacher.

The stars shine in the

night.

The stars shine in the

night.

Share your things with

others.

Share your things with

others.

I love ice cream with

chocolate sauce.

I love ice cream with

chocolate sauce.

Roses are red.

Roses are red.

Violets are blue.

Violets are blue.

Have you seen water

running?

Have you seen water

running?

Forests are full of life.

Forests are full of life.

Do not harm the animals.

Do not harm the animals.

Well Done
You are doing good.

God made the earth.

God made the earth.

children play in the park.

children play in the park.

We should grow more trees.

We should grow more trees.

A barber cuts our hair.

A barber cuts our hair.

The stream flows gently.

The stream flows gently.

Exercise keeps us fit.

Exercise keeps us fit.

Joey sits in the pouch in

its mother's belly.

Joey sits in the pouch in

its mother's belly.

Baby monkey cling to

their mothers.

Baby monkey cling to

their mothers.

Dog is my favourite

animal.

Dog is my favourite

animal.

Wash your hands before

and after eating.

Wash your hands before

and after eating.

Jams and jellies are my

favourites.

Jams and jellies are my

favourites.

Fruits should be washed

before eating.

Fruits should be washed

before eating.

A watchman guards our

house.

A watchman guards our

house.

Animals are our best

friends.

Animals are our best

friends.

My favourite sport is

football.

My favourite sport is

football.

Our teachers are good

and kind.

Our teachers are good

and kind.

It is good to greet people

when we meet them.

It is good to greet people

when we meet them.

A baby deer walks when it

is a day old.

A baby deer walks when it

is a day old.

I love to eat sweets and
chocolates.

I love to eat sweets and
chocolates.

Congratulation
You did a great job.

★ ★ ★ ★ ★

If your child likes the book,
please do leave a review on Amazon